Technical education & its need in India - Primary Source Edition

Abdul Latif

T155
L3

Sir Charles Lyall K.C.S.I.

India Office

Whitehall

London (S.W.)

England

To His Honour

Sir Charles Lyall K.C.S.I.

M.A. LLD &c

from Harinath De

Dacca. Dec. 8. 1903

N.B This as originally meant to be an address.

TECHNICAL EDUCATION
&
-- Its Need in India --

It is my conviction that so long as our race shall last, the subject of education must be one of the most important topics which shall never cease to engross its attention. With the growth of the race by virtue of education and other factors, new developments, individual, national and internationa will arise which will from time to time necessitate a rfvision of the schemes of education which have become current And besides, the share which individuals, communities and the State have to bear in forwarding the cause of education will ever be a problem which shall receive different solutions at different times and according to the points of view from which it may be looked at. So even if we have to confine ourselves to the subject of education at these fortnightly meetings there will be

lack

lack of topics to discourse upon, and I hope and trust there will be no lack of persons able and worthy to discourse upon them.

The subject of Technical Education, which is not only an absorbing topic here in India, but which is engaging the attention of all classes of men from the helmsmen of the state downwards throughout the civilized world. The agitation about technical education demonstrates the point, namely, the necessity of revision from time to time of systems of education in vogue This necessity is traceable immediately to the rivalry of the European nationalities in the matter of trades and productive industries, and this again is traceable to discoveries in Science which have a tendency to dispense with human labour.

Notwithstanding the diversities in the manner in which it is imparted or conducted in different

ages

ages and in different countries, the object of education has been the same, namely, to store the mind with knowledge. A great deal nowadays is said in condemnation of this being taken to be the object of education, and etymology is invoked to show that the object of education should be to draw out the mind, rather than to store it with knowledge. As if the mind can be drawn out or developed except by supplying it with its proper pabulum, which is knowledge. Even if it can be drawn out without knowledge, or with scanty knowledge, it will be certainly not be a healthy development. The mind under such a process will be a mere windbag capable of making much noise, but incapable of doing real, useful work While the main object of education, however, is and must be the supply of knowledge to the mind, it must not be forgotten that the quantity, the quality and the season of that supply should be regulated according to the constitution, the capacity

and the future career of the mind which has to be so supplied with. If this simple and obvious principle is kept in view the function of education will be easily understood, and will be found to include the training or disciplining of the mind so as to enable it to be self-reliant in adding to its knowledge and practical in applying its acquired knowledge to useful purposes.

It is thus with the advance of education, its function has assumed a twofold character, a general and a special training of the mind; the general applicable to all individuals, and the special adapted for those who are to pursue a particular vocation in life. Up to a very recent period the general had the predominance and the special was confined to a few subjects such as divinity, law, medicine and engineering. It is only in the most advanced countries that these special subjects have found a place in the curriculum of educational institutions. In

less advanced countries one or more or all of these subjects are left to chance and hap-hazard. Wherever these subjects have formed part of regular education, they are by common consent allowed to come only after a preliminary general training more or less complete. In other words, general education is made the basis of special education in these subjects. In the case of divinity and law the general education is required to be of a higher standard than in the case of medicine and engineering, thereby tacitly placing the latter in a lower position, though it is questionable if the highest general training is not absolutely necessary for the attainment of the highest special knowledge and training in medicine and engineering.

But the circumstances of society demand a larger supply of men with special knowledge in medicine and engineering than is possible to have, if attainment of that special knowledge were made to follow

the

the highest general knowledge. Hence, the necessity of the lowering of the general standard in order to enable men to pass on quickly to the study of the special subjects. In this fact we have the initial divergence as it were of technical (as understood in the present day) from general education It was from this fact that practical men were led to recognize the difference between the two kinds of training and to see the necessity of multiplying the subjects of special training.

The word "technical" is derived from the Greek techne, which means 'art'. Now art may have a restricted as well as a comprehensive signification. In its restricted sense it may mean the application of some particular kind of knowledge to some useful purpose in which the body, the hands in particular, is the applying agency. In this sense art deals with material things, and the instruments employed are primarily the external parts of the body. Art

may

may have a more comprehensive signification than the above, and may mean the application of knowledge to some purpose, whether that purpose be useful or not in the utilitarian sense. In this sense the work of the priest, of the lawyer, may be looked upon as art inasmuch as in the one case it is the application of the knowledge of theology for the purpose of controlling and regulating the consciences of men, and in the other the application of the knowledge of law for the purpose of maintaining justice between man and man And education itself becomes an art, the art of teaching, or the application of knowledge of the human mind and of the laws of its development and growth, for the purpose of enabling it to attain its maturity in order to fulfil its destiny in creation

cordance with the comprehen-
, has now come to mean
e technical education
ished from general edu-

education in the four special branches of knowledge mentioned above. And therefore technical education in its higher sense has been going on for centuries before the modern agitation about technical education in its lower sense had begun. The birth of technical education must have been simultaneous with the perception of difference of occupations to be pursued by different individuals. Technical education is, therefore, no new thing under the sun. Indeed, as Mr. Payne has rightly observed in his "Contributions to the Science of Education" that: "the prevailing type of education during the whole "of the historic period 'was technical or profession- "'al', its purpose being to equip men for service as agents or instruments". In Greece the object of education was "to train the mind with a view to "its conducting to a man's conception of the high- "est good, and to his ability to discharge the high- "est function of the State". In Rome it was to train an accomplished orator. In both these instan-

ces

instances the object aimed at was eminently practical.

I look upon the present agitation about technical education as the outcome of the organic growth of education in general, and as such it is not only legitimate but will prove a necessary factor in the progress of education as a whole. Technical education is no bugbear which need frighten statesmen out of their wits, or drive patriots and philanthropists into the frenzy of despair. It is easily understood, though I must say that writers about it not only here but even in England do not seem to grasp fully its scope and its requirements. "Con-"siderable misapprehensions", says Sir Philip Magnus, "still exists in the public mind as to the aims and possibilities of technical education. Some persons look to technical education to remedy all our industrial short-comings; others fail to see its advantages orits necessity. Some, again, regard all

science

science teaching as technical; others restrict the word "technical" to the teaching of an actual trade. The majority of people take a very narrow view of the extension of this term: and very few seem to understand the different kinds of training to which it is properly applicable. "I often wonder", continues he, "what kind of idea those persons can have formed who speak, and even write of teaching "technical education", and of placing it in a school cerriculum, side by side with history and geography as if it were some newly discovered branch of knowledge".

Technical education is no other than "the education which makes a man expert in his calling", whatever that may be, and as such must necessarily have "its allotted place in that wider education which makes him a worthy member of a civilized common wealth". It is a mistake on the part of the advocates of technical education to believe and to make others believe that in the circumstances of modern society it must, if not altogether, at

at least to a very large extent, supersede general education. My own impression is that the result of this agitation will be, as it has already begun to be, to render general education more general, and more comprehensive than it has hitherto been. General education upto a very recent period has been running in a very narrow groove of language, literature and philosophy, unenlightened by the advanced and advancing knowledge which has carried and is every day carrying man into the arcana of nature in all her departments.

I am fully persuaded that if instead of the attempt to stuff the mind with mere words whose signification could only be understood with difficulty in after life, an attempt which must necessarily be, and positively is disagreeable to both teacher and taught, and attended with the minimum of result, if instead of this the attempt were made to promote the contact of the mind with the

the external world so that the mind could form its own ideas of things and events, and have its perceptive, intellectual and emotional faculties thus awakened and stimulated,----I am fully persuaded that if education could be thus imparted and by competent teachers, we would by the time that we now matriculate in the university, have our minds stored with all the knowledge that any university requires of such of its candidates, and that that knowledge would be in better order and readier for use under any emergency without any great strain upon the memory, than is under the present system. The same idea finds vent from every one who has the interests of the race at heart. Mr. J. H. Gladstone one of the leading scientists of England thus express -ed it in an article in Nature. "It seems most desirable" says he, "that every child who enters our schools should be led to observe and inquire; its curiosity and activity should be encouraged and directed; only when its senses have been made

made acquainted with things should it be introduced to the words by which they are called, first orally, then in writing or print. It should proceed from the concrete to the abstract. The works of the creator are as worthy to be studied as the words of men, and should hold as high a place in any school curriculum".

Science has already forced its way into the higher curriculum of the old educational establishments of the civilized nations of the world, and if this agitation about technical education is carried on in a proper spirit and by persons competent to deal with it, the teaching of science will be found to be appropriately begun with the dawn of intelligence, and then and then ~~only~~ alone will education cease to be the aimless affair it very often now is, and adjust itself to the actual need and practical ends of life, for then science and art, theory and practice, will be harmoniously blended in all our educational institutions from the highest to the lowest. But "we must again and again repeat", in the words of Mr Montague, "that neither elementary education nor technical education can be perfected apart from education in general".

Mr. Montague has very properly observed that "the strength of Germany lies in the culture of every class of Germans, in the real love of learning which animates the people and their rulers, in the patient, inquiring

and scientific spirit which has transformed almost every branch of human activity from metaphysics to the arts of war".

So that, it is the most cultured, the most generally educated nation in Europe which excels all others in technical education. And indeed it is the fact, that the success of special or technical education for the higher profession depends upon its being based upon a high standard of general education, that has led to the present demand for systematic technical education for the lower profes-sions or trades. These lower professions or trades however necessary, nay absolutely necessary, to the very existence of society, were looked down upon in ancient times, and till within a recent period, as degrading occupations, unworthy of being followed by the higher ranks, by the favoured, the educated few Hence they were not deemed to be fit subjects of instruction in schools which import general instruction as well as special instruction in the higher professions. Neverthless, they were not, and

at haphazard. They were taught practically by men who were carrying them on, that is, by men who had hemselves become experts in them. How far the value of technical education for such trades was appreciated in this country in ancient times (during the Hindu Period) will be seen from the fact of the caste system, by which particular arts were not only specialized but confined to heriditary classes so as to ensure training in those arts from the earliest years of life. But the fact that the hereditary classes or castes which followed these professions or trades were looked upon as being in the lowest scale of society, shows the estimation in which the trades were held, and shows also what mean ideas of education were entertained by the enlightened men of olden times, and what unworthy conception they had of the dignity of human labour.

This primitive mode of technical education

education in the lower trades and arts did suffice so long as things remained in <u>statusquo,</u> so long as human labour was the sole factor in the carrying on of the trade and in the execution of the art. But man is a progressive animal pre-eminently in Europe, though unfortunately not so in our part of the world. While in Asia, therefore, things have remained in <u>statusquo</u> for centuries, in Europe they have been continually changing, thanks to the continual advance of knowledge penetrating the secrets of nature. One discovery was made which completely altered the aspect of the trades and the industries. This was the discovery of the properties of steam which has led to the invention of labour-saving machinery and which in its turn has effected a revolution in the mode of production, called into existence new industries, and given rise to marvellous facilities in locomotion unknown before. "Nearly all the differences", says Sir Philip, "tnat distinguish produc-

tive industry and mercantile business as pursued to-day and a century ago, are referable to these two causes. The arts both of production and distribution have become more scientific, and dependent to a great extent upon acquired knowledge and skill than upon unaided native intelligence. One feature of these changed conditions is, that the knowledge, and in some cases, the skill, which are now needed for industrial purposes, can no longer be adequately obtained in the actual practice of a trade, but require, as in the cases of law and medicine, a preliminary training, or specialised school instruction".

"We might if time served, trace back to the steam engine many of the changes, which during the last thirty years, have been creeping over our educational system, changes which mark only the beginning of a revolution that promises to sweep away much that is time-honoured in our

our methods of instruction. The wave that is pushing forward technical education will not subside until our primary middle schools, our higher secondary schools as well as our ancient universities shall have felt its influence".

From the preliminary observations that have been already made it will be evident that the whole problem of technical education, in the restricted or lower sense in which it is now used, resolves itself into the question, — Whether the mass of human beings, the majority of our fellow creatures, who are engaged in the production of the necessaries and the luxuries of life are to remain in ignorance or are to be educated, and if educated whether the education that they receive is to be an unmeaning and aimless one as hitherto, or to be adapted to their future career; in otherwords, whether the old barbarism which has become stereotyped in the caste system among Hindus of our country, and

and which is continuing in the present day throughout the world in some form or other, by which the community is divided into two classes, a favoured, cultured, educated class and a degraded, uncultured, illiterate class, whether this barbarism is to be perpetuated, or whether a better, a purer, a holier state of things is to take its place, by which every man that is born, in whatever rank of life, is to be allowed every opportunity and facility for developing his faculties so as to fulfil his destiny in creation. The proper solution of the problem has long since been arrived at on the continent of Europe, and conservative England has at last awakened from its slumber of delusive security, originating in the lower plane of the interests of the trading classes, the demand for technical education has passed to the higher plane of the interests of the state. For it is no longer a question, whether

— for want of proper technical education a few individuals, or a few trading and mercantile firms will suffer, but it is a question, in view of the keen competition that has necessarily followed new discoveries and new inventions, whether a nation can now safely neglect technical education as part of national education without detriment to its trades, industries, and manufactures. And this demand has to pass on to the highest plane, the plane of philanthropy, in order to receive its due and complete answer.

I have made this last remark advisedly. For however easy of understanding the meaning of technical education is, as I have said before, the organization of technical education into a system is far from easy, indeed, is the most difficult task which can engage the attention of the educationist, of the community and of the state. Technical education, we have seen to be that education which has reference to the future career of the person who receives it, which, in other words, would enable him to be expert in the calling he is to follow. Now think for a moment of the future careers of the rising generation, think of the numbers of callings which await the individuals of a community, and you will at once realise the difficulty, the intricacy and the magnitude of the task set before you of organising a system which will be suitable for all carrers for all [illegible], [illegible] that

veries in science leading to fresh inventions in art. No wonder that some people should have denounced the demand for technical education as a vague one. "The cry for technical education is 'vague'", says the authority already quoted, "because it has a different significance according to the source from which it emanates. It means one thing to the workman and another to the foreman, and, again something different to the manager or manufacturer. It is not the same in reference to handwork as to machinework, and it changes again when considered in connection with scientific invention or artistic design. Those who think of technical education in relation to any single industry fail to understand the meaning of the cry that is raised by those who are engaged in other trades."

Technical education [illegible] great divisions, [illegible] be

in manufactures, mining, building and similar occupations, and the education of those who will be engaged in agriculture. Each of these principal divisions may again be subdivided into three grades: the primary, the intermediate, and the advanced. In each of these grades the instruction must be varied according to the nature of the particular branch of industry which is taught. By primary instruction is understood such technical instruction as is required by the ordinary artizan.

"The intermediate technical instruction is an instruction for students of many descriptions, for that minority of gifted workmen whose talents claim more than elementary training, for managers of departments in large works, for heads of establishment who lack time, means, and inclination for an elaborate culture, and for merchants and distributors who find their advantage in having some theoretical k[illegible] traf-

fic. Schools for imparting such instruction may be roughly classified as follows:- I. Schools giving general technical instruction, ranking above the apprenticeship schools and below the high schools such as German Poly-technics. II. Schools giving instruction in particular industries, as building, mining, weaving. III. Schools of industrial art.

The highest grade of technical education, differs widely in its circumstances from the lower grades. The object is twofold; first to supply the national industries with the needful staff of experts in applied science, and secondly to supply competent teachers to intermediate technical schools. In providing for advanced technical instruction, the essential thing is to have a high standard. To try to make in[illegible]

too

too impatient for results, to exclude the Spirit of research and the love of science -- this is the certain means to make it poor, shallow, imfruitful, and, in the strictest sense useless. The noblest type of such a school is to be found in the Polytechnics of Germanyand Switzerland".

Technical education in agriculture, especially of the advanced kind, is of the utmost importance, in as much as on agriculture depends the life of man. Failure in agriculture means famine, desolution and death to thousands and millions and the noblest work of Science consists in rendering agriculture the most succesful persuit, rendering it as much as possible independent of the freaks and caprices of Nature.

If,

If you have realized what the intricacy and the magnitude of a system of technical education must be, you will not fail to realise at the same time what the cost of such an organization is likely to be. A few figures collected by the Royal Commission on Technical Instruction will give you an idea of the enormous cost at which technical schools and colleges are being maintained in Germany and other countries on the continent of Europe.

"The Munich Technical High School cost £157,000, the apparatus alone being worth £36,000, and the annual expenses amounting to £20,000. The Zurich Polytechnic spends £20,000, annually, £13800 being derived from Federal taxes, and £3794 only from fees. There are fortyfive professors on the lecturing st[illegible] [illegible] a

state sub-vention of £12,000, that of Dresden £12,200. The Hanover Polytechnic cost £350,000; its collection of models (highly engineering), £36,000, and £1250 is spent every year in adding to the collection. The Berlin Polytechnic cost £450,000; that of Moscow £496,000."

You will now understand why I said that the demand for technical education must pass on to the highest plane, the plane of philanthropy, in order to receive its complete realisation. Where is this enormous cost to come from? If from Government, it will mean additional taxation, and all taxation means grinding of the poor, for whose benefit chiefly, the demand for technical education is made. The money ought, in my humble opinion, to come from the rich for whose benefit the poor

labour with the sweat of their brow. Ours is a poor country, but there is in it, still a large amount of hoarded wealth. "And a most urgent need in India, therefore," as Mr. Cotton well observed in his Address on Technical education at the Bethune Society, "a most urgent need in India, therefore, is the better disposition of hoarded wealth. India is in need of wealthy men who have wisdom and experience, who will not fritter away their money on tamasha and ceremonies, and who are not unwilling to lay out capital on undertakings which will bring them neither titles nor official smiles. We do not want capital to be buried, we do not want it to be wasted on marriage expenses, nor do we want it to be squandered in sycophantic subscriptions or in the reception and entertainment of officials. Some expenditure of this [illegible] able

but the waste which now runs rampant must be checked. No spectacle is more deplorable in the eyes of the well-wishers of this poor country than the lavish squandering outlay which fashion demands and public opinion sanctions on these occasions."

Vast and intricate as must be a complete system of technical education, it has been shown by all authorities competent to judge on the subject that the existing system of education may be so modified as to avoid the necessity of creating separate schools and thus considerably reduce the initial cost. All that is necessary for this purpose is to introduce drawing and science teaching into all primary schools, not as optional but as compulsory subjects. And now the public are to be [illegible]

desideratum been lately fulfilled. The difficulty experienced by school authorities even in England is in the procuring of competent Science teachers. But with the demand supply will come. In our country the difficulty is infinitely greater than in England, and it was to overcome this difficulty that the Science Association was established. under the recognised leadership of such a master-mind as Dr. Mohendra Lal Sircar. If the institution had been duly patronized and supported, the cause of technical education would have been greatly advanced by it. But the country has not yet realized its importance and its requirements, and it is barely keeping up its existence by the utmost economy of the scanty funds placed at its disposal. Imagine what must be the enlightenment of a country which is

is never tired of boasting of its high education, when with the paltrysum of a lac and a quarter rupees the Science Association was expected to do what Europe has done with its rich endowments for science and technology.

Messrs. Eliot and Pedlar, in their Memorandum on Technical Education for Bengal, have very properly observed that of the two classes of instruction, higher and lower, the higher must necessarily be commenced first inorder to provide teachers for the lower Course. In no country, in fact, can technical education be properly, efficiently and permanently carried on by indigenous efforts, without a previous supply of indigenous scientific teachers. Thus, apart from all other considerations, we have in the very requirements of technical education, a powerful argument for the necessity of a pure Science institution. [illegible] well to

to leave the cultivation of Science unhampered with thoughts of immediate practical utility. For as Helmhottz has wisely said, "Whoever, in the pursuit of science, seeks after immediate practical utility, may generally rest assured that he will seek in vain." It is enough that "We are convinced that whatever contributes to the knowledge of the forces of nature or the powers of the human mind is worth cherishing, and may in its own one time, bear practical fruit, very often where we should least have expected it."

information can be obtained at www.ICGtesting.com
the USA
342030815
V00015B/286/P